GLOBAL PRODUCTS

Cars

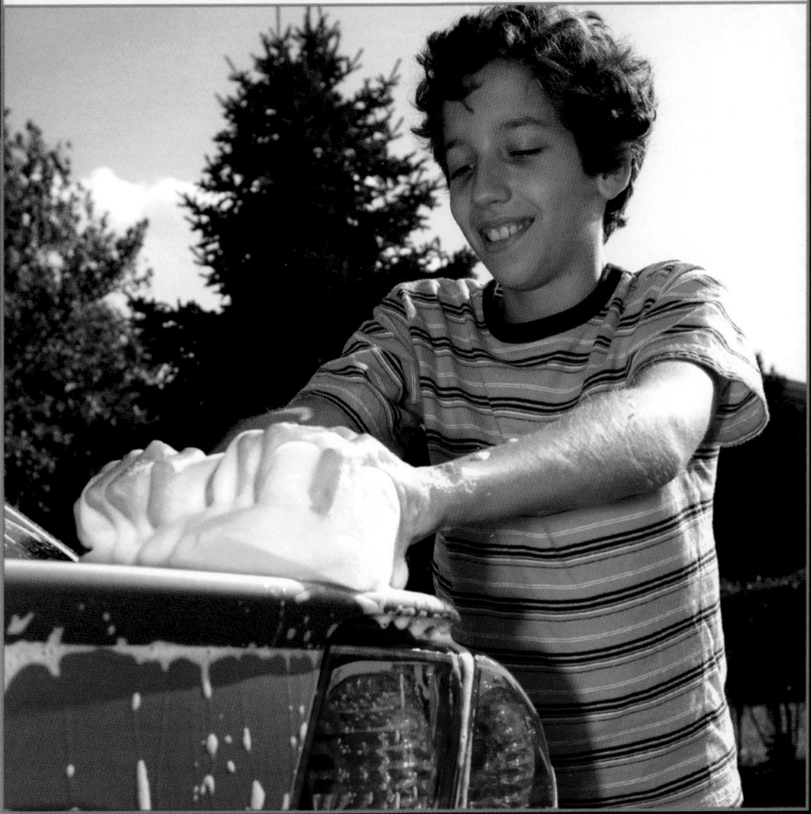

Robert Green

Cherry Lake Publishing
Ann Arbor, Michigan

Published in the United States of America by Cherry Lake Publishing
Ann Arbor, MI
www.cherrylakepublishing.com

Content Adviser: Edward Kolodziej, Director of Global Studies, University of Illinois, Champaign, Illinois

Photo Credits: pages 9, 21, © Bettmann/CORBIS; page 14, © TWPhoto/CORBIS; page 18, © Michael S. Yamashita/CORBIS; page 19, © Danny Lehman/CORBIS; page 23, © Charles O'Rear/CORBIS

Map by XNR Productions Inc.

Library of Congress Cataloging-in-Publication Data
Green, Robert, 1969–
Cars / by Robert Green.
p. cm. — (Global products)
ISBN-13: 978-1-60279-028-5
ISBN-10: 1-60279-028-0
1. Automobile industry and trade—Juvenile literature. 2. Automobiles—Design and construction—Juvenile literatre. 3. Globalization—Juvenile literature. I. Title. II. Series.

HD9710.A2G74 2008
338.4'7629222—dc22 2007003897

Cherry Lake Publishing would like to acknowledge the work of The Partnership for 21st Century Skills.
Please visit www.21stcenturyskills.org *for more information.*

Table of Contents

CHAPTER ONE

An Incredible Journey

You can see rows of new cars at a new car dealership.

When twelve-year-old Katzutaka Ito was awakened by his grandfather, he rubbed his eyes and yawned widely. He had promised to go with his grandfather to buy a new car for the family. But at that early hour, when the fog was still sleeping in the valleys of Japan, he wondered what was so important about a car anyway.

Grandfather told him that he had no idea just how lucky he was to grow up in a rich Japan. "Japan was not always like this," he said. "After the war, we had no cars and no gasoline. Our lives were ruined, and the economy was in shambles."

Katzutaka, having only known the prosperity of life in Japan today, yawned again. It was just another of his grandfather's stories about World War II, a time he could hardly imagine. Katzutaka thought about it for a little bit and replied, "But grandfather, aren't cars everywhere in Japan, and doesn't Japan ship cars to places all over the world?"

"Yes, of course," Katzutaka's grandfather answered. "But Japan's rise to a car-manufacturing powerhouse is a remarkable story, and so too is the story of the car itself."

In fact, it's an incredible journey that involves continuing technological innovations and the emergence of a vast and complex global industry. Not only are Japan's cars being **exported** to countries around the world, as Katzutaka said, they are also **manufactured** in different places around the world.

Although buying a car is typically done at a dealership close to home, the car is the product of a global process that involves materials, parts, and people from around the world. This is known as **globalization**. When Katzutaka accompanies his grandfather to buy a new car, he is experiencing a global phenomenon, whether he knows it or not, just as a car buyer would in the United States.

Katzutaka was now fascinated by his grandfather's knowledge and wanted to learn more about the history of the automobile. Suddenly, there were so many questions running through his head that he could barely keep them all in order! Katzutaka blurted out the first question that came to mind.

Busy highways such as this one were unheard of 100 years ago.

"Grandfather, what is so important about the car anyway?"

Grandfather smiled and replied with a question of his own.

"People are made with legs that can carry them from one place to another, right?" he asked.

Katzutaka giggled at this question and replied, "Yes, Grandfather, of course!"

His grandfather went on to explain, "To travel longer distances, people in the past often used animals. In the United States, a horse could take a mail carrier delivering letters to towns across the American West. In deserts, riders mounted camels that, unlike horses, were able to stand the heat and needed water less frequently. A prince in India or Southeast Asia could even ride on an elephant. But people continued to search for cheaper and faster ways to travel long distances, because feeding an elephant could be expensive. Besides, elephants never really traveled very fast anyway!"

Katzutaka understood everything his grandfather was explaining to him, but he still wanted to know more about the history of the automobile.

"So what is the story behind the car?" asked Katzutaka. As the two of them walked to the car dealership, Grandfather explained the history of the car in great detail.

~

A primary reason why goods can be made all over the world today is the low cost of shipping. While most people travel across the seas by airplane, goods still cross the seas to their destinations by ship. Ships are slower, but they are cheaper. Every day, ships crisscross the oceans carrying automobiles and automobile parts.

A technological invention allowed people to make a machine to get them from one point to another more quickly and efficiently, without relying on animals. This was the automobile, or what we commonly call the car. Long before the car, people had used wheels to move heavy objects. They used wheelbarrows to carry loads too heavy for one person. And horses pulled wheeled carts and buggies. But what if those wheeled vehicles could be made to move without humans or animals pushing or pulling them?

In 1885, an enterprising German named Karl Benz—whose name still adorns the Mercedes-Benz automobile—invented an automobile powered by a gasoline engine. The engine propelled a car by burning gasoline in a complicated process known as internal combustion. But there was more refining to be done before the internal combustion engine could be mass-produced, and European and American inventors worked on perfecting it.

Karl Benz invented this automobile in 1885 and called it the Benz Patent Motorwagen.

With the invention of the internal combustion engine, car designers set to work developing ideas that would bring the car to average people. Now, cars shape the landscape of the world we live in—think of the many roads that crisscross a single town. And the car industry has given rise to a global industry that relies on the work of people in many countries to build a single automobile that is purchased close to home.

CHAPTER TWO

Tires in Motion

Tires are just one of the many parts that make up cars.

Katzutaka was fascinated. "Grandfather, where do we get all of our car parts from?" he asked.

Grandfather thought about this for a bit and then began explaining the idea of **specialization** and the concept of globalization to his grandson.

Over time, car manufacturers discovered that it was often cheaper to make car parts in different places and ship them to a factory where they would be assembled to make a car. This might seem strange, since it takes time and money to ship things from one place to another, but the key to this phenomenon is specialization. Certain companies became very good at making a single car part at a relatively low cost. Carmakers could purchase this part from the company more cheaply than they could make the part themselves. This allowed carmakers to produce less-expensive cars and keep costs down.

If we look at a single car part, such as the tire, it becomes clear how complicated car manufacturing has become. Without the tire, traveling in a car would be terribly uncomfortable. The tire helps to cushion the ride, making it less bumpy. Tires also provide traction to help the car grip the road. The traction provided by a tire allows for driving in rain or snow with greater safety.

Adam Smith (1723–1790) was a famous British **economist**. He observed and wrote about specialization—the dividing up of manufacturing steps.

Smith used the example of a pin factory making pins in two different ways. In the first way, each pin maker made pins from beginning to end, shaping the point and fashioning it into its final shape through a number of separate steps. In the second way, each pin maker did only one part of the process and handed the pin to the next person to do the next step. Each worker specialized in one step in the process. Smith discovered that the second method produced more pins much faster. This specialization has become the model for car manufacturers around the globe.

Another basic economic principle is known as economy of scale. This principle states that when a company makes more of a product, the cost of making the product generally decreases. This helps to explain why many companies specialize in making a single product.

The tire may look simple, but its appearance is deceiving. Rubber is the main raw material of the tire, but the rubber is treated by complex chemical processes. There is also a layer of fabric and wire within the tire to give it strength.

Natural rubber comes from rubber trees. The sap of rubber trees is harvested at rubber plantations—places where forests of rubber trees are planted. The sap that comes from the trees is called latex, and it oozes from a tapped tree much like sap from a maple tree, which is used to make maple syrup. A bucket collects the dripping latex, which is then shipped to a factory for processing into natural rubber.

Rubber trees once grew only in Africa and South American countries such as Brazil. The British transported the tree to southern and Southeast Asia, and today, those areas are the prime source of natural rubber. In Malaysia, for example, rubber plantations produce a huge amount of revenue for the country.

Latex drips into a container attached to a rubber tree on a plantation in Vietnam.

The natural rubber is then shipped to manufacturing plants all over the world to make rubber products, such as tires, carpentry tools, and roof-gutter linings. Rubber from Malaysia loaded onto ships might pass through major Asian port cities nearby, such as Hong Kong or Singapore, before reaching a processing or manufacturing center in Japan, the United States, or elsewhere in the world.

A company that specializes in the making of tires will generally also make other rubber products. This is because once a steady supply of raw materials—in this case, rubber—is secured, it is easy for the company to make many products out of the rubber. This is known as diversification—making different types of things. Diversification allows companies to make money from different products and keep profits up, even if one product is not selling

CHAPTER THREE

From the Plantation to the Factory

"So car parts from different factories are shipped to one big factory, where they're all put together as one car?" asked Katzutaka.

"Precisely!" replied his grandfather. "Different companies specialize in different parts. Then, after the cars have been assembled at the factory, the company loads the new cars onto containerships to be shipped all over the world."

A car is loaded onto a cargo ship in Japan.

"But Grandfather," asked Katzutaka, "tell me more about tires. Who specializes in tires, and what happens to the rubber once it gets to the manufacturing plant?" Katzutaka was intrigued by the **technology** of the tire. Grandfather began to explain the process of how tires are made from the raw rubber and other materials.

~

Tire companies, like car companies, are worldwide enterprises. Goodyear, a major U.S. manufacturer of tires, has facilities for making tires or tire parts all over the world. Aside from its many sites in the United States, Goodyear makes tires in various countries in Europe and South America, in the African nations of Morocco and South Africa, and in New Zealand and Australia. In Asia alone, where most rubber comes from, Goodyear makes tires in at least nine countries.

A tire is more than just the rubber that goes into it. Goodyear also has factories that make just one part of a tire, for tires that will then be assembled at a different place. In Asheboro, North Carolina, for example, Goodyear has a plant that makes the steel wire that adds strength to the finished tire. In Melbourne, Australia, and Bangkok, Thailand, the company has plants that create tire treads, the pattern on the outside of the tire that allows it to better grip the road. In the Southeast Asian nation of Singapore, which is close to the rubber plantations, Goodyear has a center for purchasing rubber as well as laboratories for testing and research.

The reason these factories are spread all over the globe is a complex story. Having a rubber-purchasing center near a supply of rubber makes sense—transporting the rubber is simpler. Companies must balance other factors as well. Factories needing unskilled **labor** can be located in places where there are many workers willing to do jobs that don't require previous experience. This type of job doesn't pay as well as jobs requiring higher skill levels. But when skilled labor—requiring much training and experience—is needed to perform certain difficult procedures, those factories are often situated where skilled workers can be found. The companies, in other words, think

Bicycle tires are another product made by rubber manufacturers.

globally and seek out the natural benefits of different geographic areas and their populations.

So, tires are a global product, with Goodyear and other tire manufacturers making tires or tire parts all over the world and selling them in local **markets** or shipping them abroad. This model, however, developed only over time.

When Goodyear began producing tires in 1898, the company had only thirteen workers. The company didn't make automobile tires back then. Instead, it made money from the rising popularity of bicycles, which use rubber tires, too. Goodyear also made solid rubber tires for carriages and even rubber poker chips. As the demand for car tires increased, however, the company began to operate facilities abroad, in many cases closer to either the natural resources that went into the products or the customers the company wished to sell to. Today, Goodyear operates more than 100 plants in 29 countries. It ships tires to car manufacturers' factories, where they are put onto the cars we drive.

Many executives live abroad or frequently travel abroad. They are the people who make decisions and help run multinational companies, which have divisions spread around the globe. Executives once spent most of their lives in offices near their homes, but global manufacturing now requires managers who are comfortable traveling to other countries and working with people from other places. What kinds of skills do you think someone needs to work in a country far from home?

CHAPTER FOUR

ENTER THE JAPANESE

A woman works on a Toyota assembly line in Japan.

"Wow, so Goodyear even made rubber poker chips?" asked Katzutaka.

"It most certainly did, and it continues to be the world's biggest seller of rubber automobile tires," replied Katzutaka's grandfather.

"Grandfather, how did Japan become so well known for making cars?" asked Katzutaka.

"It didn't happen right away," Grandfather replied. "Japanese auto manufacturers were dealing with a tight market. There were many competitors in the United States and Europe. At first, it was very hard to compete, but soon Japanese companies managed to develop great products and ship cars all over the world."

Facilities dedicated to the design, production, assembly, and distribution of cars are located around the world. There was a time when cars were largely manufactured in Europe and the United States, even though the raw materials came from all over the world. Eventually, carmakers sought to produce cars more cheaply in other countries. The lower costs resulted from the lower wages paid to people who worked in factories there.

This General Motors assembly line in the United States looks a lot like auto assembly lines in Japan and around the world.

The costs of labor differ from country to country. A country in which labor costs are higher—where workers receive higher wages—is typically richer, with an advanced economy. Countries that have lower labor costs are still developing economically and socially, and people there are willing to work for less money. Multinational companies have an incentive to locate their factories in places where labor costs are lower. This helps keep the price of goods down and also helps employ people who need work.

When companies seek cheaper labor in different countries, jobs move. Workers in the United States auto industry still face this problem today. As companies hire workers overseas, they hire fewer workers at home. The effects on the economy are mixed. Workers, especially unskilled factory workers, often find themselves without jobs and must find new ones. But **consumers** can buy products, such as cars and goods in stores, for less money.

As North American and European carmakers spread their manufacturing plants around the world, the know-how to make a car also spread. After World War II, the Japanese began to produce cars in Japan after learning how from the American companies that had plants there. At first, Japanese cars were sold locally. But the cars, which were smaller and less expensive, were soon in demand in other countries.

In the 1970s, the United States faced an oil crisis that drove up the price of gasoline. As the price rose, consumers bought smaller cars that burned less gas and offered greater mileage per gallon of gas. Many of these cars were Japanese, and the number of Japanese cars sold in the United States rose dramatically. Today, more cars and trucks are produced in Japan than any other country except the United States. One Japanese company alone, Toyota, makes more passenger cars per year than any other company in the world. (General Motors, a U.S. company, makes more vehicles if trucks are included.)

As the number of Japanese cars rose, however, many Americans worried that the U.S. car industry would be hurt and people would lose jobs to foreign competitors. But globalization changed the entire nature of production and made the car's origin much less important.

Cars line up at a gas station in California during the gasoline shortage in the late 1970s.

After World War II, Japan was very poor. Much of its economy was destroyed in the war, and Japan has always lacked natural resources. But the people of Japan were good at adapting. They learned the techniques of modern manufacturing from U.S. and other foreign companies. Today, Japan has the second-largest economy in the world.

Just as the Japanese once learned techniques from foreign companies, workers in other countries today are learning from Japan. Throughout Asia, companies have benefited from the high level of Japanese investment and the many Japanese factories around the region.

For example, Toyota, Japan's largest carmaker, discovered it was cheaper to produce cars in other countries instead of in Japan. In addition, the United States and Europe threatened to place **tariffs** and **quotas** on cars imported from Japan, which made Japanese manufacturers realize that they would have to move some of their production to these countries. In the United States today, Toyota manufactures cars or car parts in eight locations. In Kentucky, the Toyota factory employs almost 7,000 people. Although competition is still a factor, it is much less important now that foreign carmakers employ local workers, just as U.S. carmakers employ people from other countries in their overseas plants.

In total, Toyota has 52 overseas manufacturing sites located in 27 countries. This means that while the brand name is Japanese, the manufacturing of Toyota cars is a truly global enterprise, making use of the skills of workers all around the world.

CHAPTER FIVE

THINKING GLOBALLY

"So Japanese carmakers actually learned how to make better cars from U.S. carmakers?" asked Katzutaka, amazed.

"Japanese automakers studied the methods used by U.S. automakers and began adopting some of the manufacturing methods used by the Americans. Over time they learned how to make better cars more efficiently," said Grandfather proudly.

Katzutaka and his grandfather were nearing the car dealership, but Katzutaka asked his grandfather to explain one more thing to him.

Toyota employees examine a car on an assembly line in Durban, South Africa.

"Grandfather, how are the Americans and the Japanese able to work with each other and learn from each other from so far away and while speaking different languages?"
he asked.

"It's because we live in a global economy," explained his grandfather. "The countries rely on each other when building and selling cars. Therefore, it is necessary for both sides to find a way to work together."

When the Japanese began to open factories in the United States, many Americans were wary of working for a foreign employer who neither looked like them nor spoke the same language. The culture of the workplace was very different in Japan and the United States.

To create a bridge between Japanese companies and American workers, the Japanese invited some of the workers to Japan to experience the Japanese way of production. The Americans were typically highly individualistic and liked to speak their minds. They discovered that the Japanese value harmony and cooperation in the workplace. Japanese workers were encouraged to express opinions, especially if they had suggestions for improvements in car design and production processes. They were also expected to respect the company's management and rules.

Unlike American workers, Japanese workers exercise together in the morning, much as you might do in gym class. The exercise is intended to create a sense of identity as a group. Many Japanese employees even spend their vacations together. In the past, many worked for the same company for their entire lives, but that is slowly changing.

Japanese carmakers and American workers have been working together for several decades. Today, there is less worry over working with foreign companies. The entire manufacturing process is spread all over the world, so there has been a gradual shift to mutual understanding and adaptation. Most of the products we use in daily life are made abroad—or parts of them are made abroad—and many people from other countries use products made in the United States.

Although the United States and Japan remain the two largest car-manufacturing countries, people in other countries also make automobiles. A South Korean manufacturer, for example,

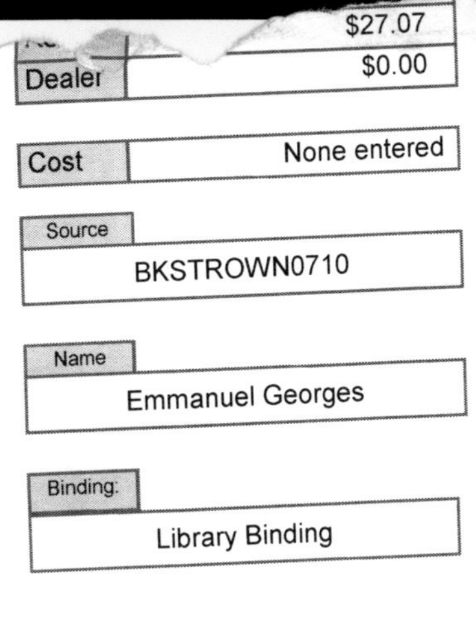

skill in today's global marketplace.

makes the Hyundai line of cars, which has become popular around the globe. Brazil is a major car manufacturing center in South America.

Gasoline is not the only energy source for today's automobiles. Brazilian auto manufacturers have been particularly successful experimenting with alternative fuels to power cars. Engines can be converted to run on ethanol—a type of grain alcohol. In Brazil, this fuel source is made from the country's sugarcane crops. In the United States, ethanol is made from corn.

New technologies are shared among countries, and new ideas, articles, and research are able to

Sometimes farmers in a country produce more of a particular crop than they can sell to consumers. In the United States, where farmers often grow too much corn, they are now able to sell corn to ethanol producers. In Brazil and other countries where sugarcane is plentiful, the production of ethanol using sugarcane is providing a boon to sugarcane farmers. The advantage of this alternative type of fuel, which can be mixed with gasoline, is that car engines can be easily converted to use the new fuel.

Sugarcane is just one crop that can be used to produce ethanol.

spread faster because of the **Internet**. The Internet has also made it easier for car manufacturers to coordinate factories all over the world. Orders are placed electronically, and factories produce only what is needed. The Internet allows manufacturers to more exactly meet the demands of consumers. They are able reduce the number of cars or car parts that have to be stocked in warehouses and car dealerships.

~

As the car dealer handed Katzutaka's grandfather the keys to his new car, Katzutaka had one last question: "Grandfather, how come you know so much about cars?"

Grandfather smiled and answered, "Because once, a long time ago, I too was a worker in an American car factory here."

Katzutaka, eyes wide open now, got into the car next to his grandfather and buckled his seat belt. As they drove home in the new car, the boy marveled that he had learned something new about cars and about his grandfather, all on the same day!

Top 10 Vehicle-Producing Countries (2005)

United States
Japan
Germany
China
South Korea
France
Spain
Canada
Brazil
United Kingdom

(source: *Ward's Automotive Yearbook 2006*)

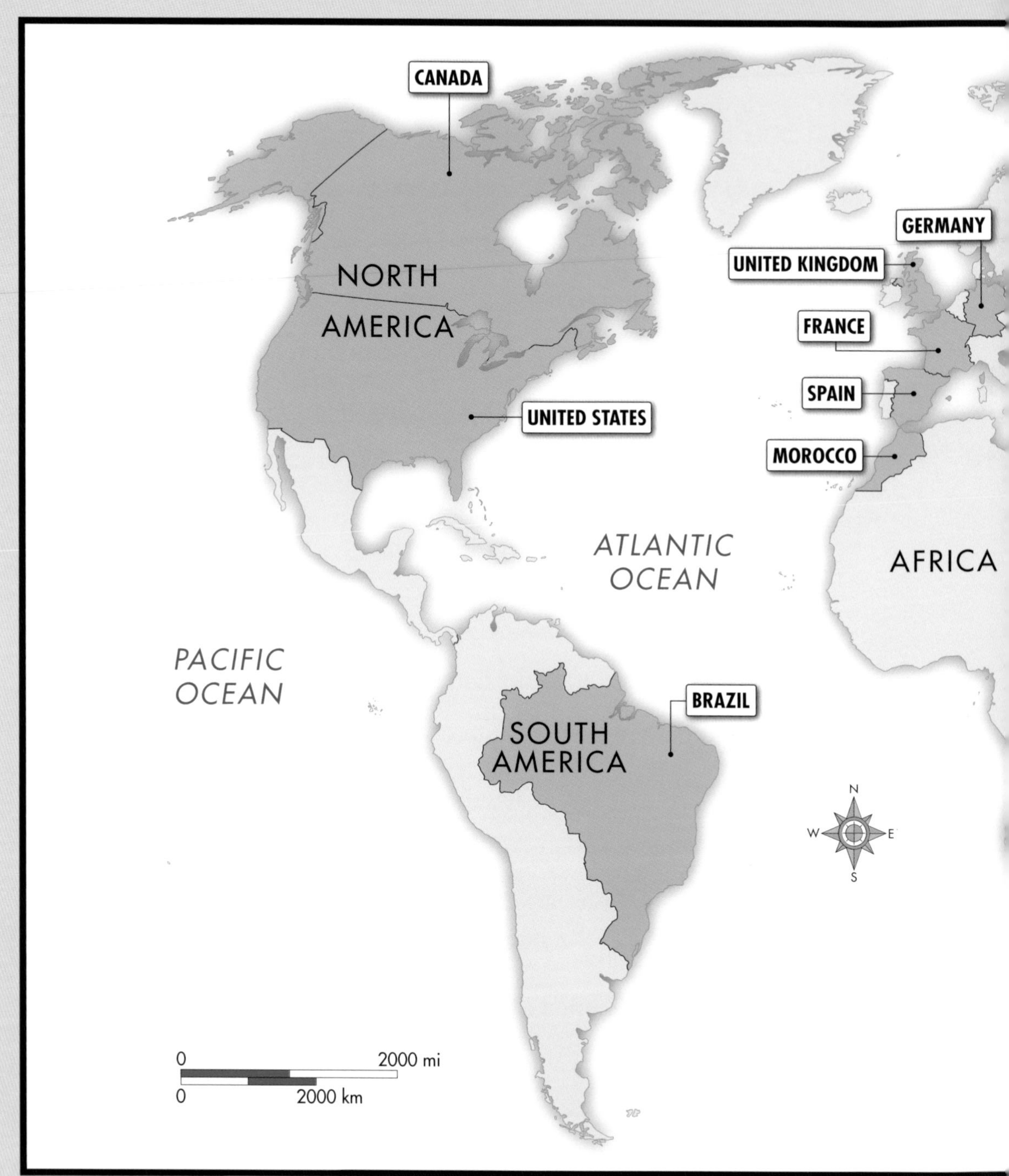

This map shows the countries and cities mentioned in the text.

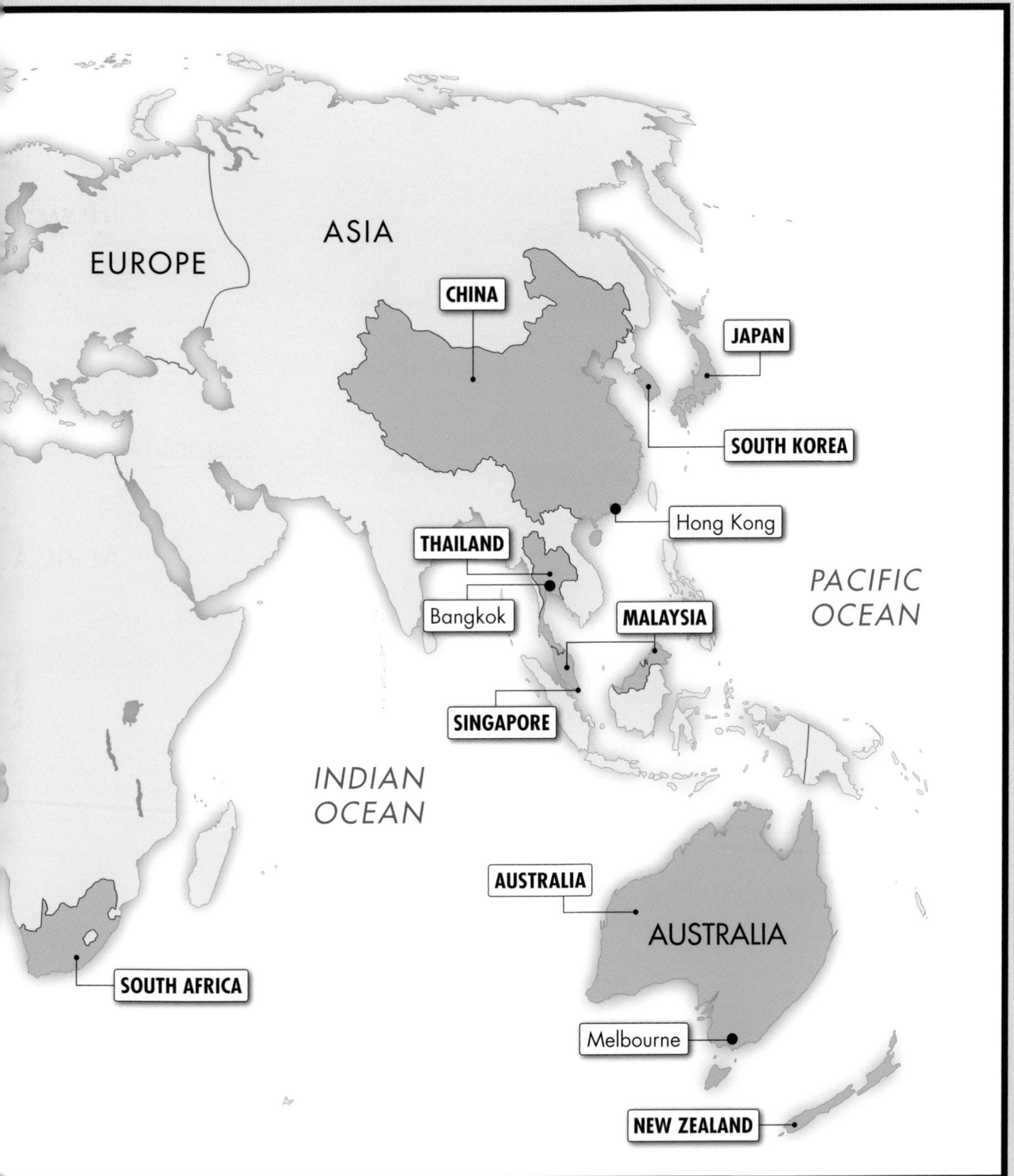

They are all places involved in the business of making and selling cars.

Glossary

consumers (kuhn-SOO-murz) people who buy and use products and services

diversification (di-VUR-suh-fuh-KAY-shun) the making of a variety of products

economist (ee-KON-uh-mist) someone who studies the production, distribution, and consumption of goods and services in a society

exported (ek-SPORT-ed) sent (as in products) to another country to be sold there

globalization (glo-buh-luh-ZAY-shun) the growing interconnection between economies around the world

goods (GUDZ) things that are sold or things that are owned by someone

Internet (IN-tur-net) an electronic network that connects computers around the world

labor (LAY-bur) a group of workers who work for wages

manufactured (man-yuh-FAK-churd) made something, usually on a large scale

markets (MAR-kits) places where goods are sold

quotas (KWOH-tuhz) fixed amounts or shares of something

specialization (spesh-uh-li-ZAY-shun) the act of focusing on a particular part of a process

tariffs (TARE-iffs) taxes on products brought in from another country

technology (tek-NOL-uh-jee) the application of science and engineering to the process of making products

For More Information

Books

Conley, Robyn. *The Automobile.* New York: Franklin Watts, 2005.

Heinrichs, Ann. *Japan.* New York: Children's Press, 2006.

Web Sites

Energy Information Administration: Energy Kid's Page—Ethanol Timeline
www.eia.doe.gov/kids/history/timelines/ethanol.html
For a timeline that outlines the development of ethanol

HowStuffWorks: How Car Engines Work
auto.howstuffworks.com/engine.htm
For an introduction to how car engines work

Index

About the Author

Kevin Cunningham is the author of several books, including biographies of Joseph Stalin and J. Edgar Hoover and a series on diseases in human history. He lives in Chicago.